Big Red Farm

Special thanks to our advisers for their expertise:

Linda Frichtel, Design Adjunct Faculty
Minneapolis College of Art & Design

Susan Kesselring, M.A., Literacy Educator
Rosemount–Apple Valley–Eagan (Minnesota) School District

PiCTURE WiNDOW BOOKS
Minneapolis, Minnesota

by Christianne C. Jones ... illustrated by Todd Ouren

Editor: Jill Kalz
Designer: Amy Muehlenhardt
Page Production: Brandie Shoemaker
Art Director: Nathan Gassman
The illustrations in this book were created digitally.

Picture Window Books
5115 Excelsior Boulevard
Suite 232
Minneapolis, MN 55416
877-845-8392
www.picturewindowbooks.com

Printed in the United States of America.

Library of Congress Cataloging-in-Publication Data
Jones, Christianne C.
Big red farm / by Christianne C. Jones ; illustrated by
Todd Ouren.
p. cm. — (Know your colors)
Includes bibliographical references and index.
ISBN-13: 978-1-4048-3110-0 (library binding)
ISBN-10: 1-4048-3110-X (library binding)
ISBN-13: 978-1-4048-3493-4 (paperback)
ISBN-10: 1-4048-3493-1 (paperback)
1. Red—Juvenile literature. 2. Color—Juvenile literature.
3. Toy and movable books—Specimens. I. Ouren, Todd, ill.
II. Title.
QC495.5.J656 2007
535.6—dc22   2006027236

The world is filled with COLORS.

RED

ORANGE

YELLOW

GREEN

BLUE

PURPLE

Colors are either primary or secondary. Red, yellow, and blue are primary colors. These are the colors that can't be made by mixing two other colors together. Orange, purple, and green are secondary colors. Secondary colors are made by mixing together two primary colors.

Black and white are neutral colors. They are used to make other colors lighter or darker.

Primary colors

Secondary colors

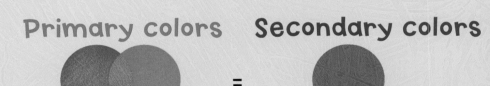

Blue + Red = Purple

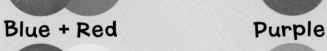

Blue + Yellow = Green

Yellow + Red = Orange

Keep your eyes open for colorful fun!

4

The color RED works hard on the farm.
It brightens up the land and adds lots of charm.

5

6

A big RED barn shines in the sun.

The **RED**-haired farmer has just begun.

9

10

The useful **RED** wagon is loaded with hay.

The noisy RED truck chug-chugs away.

12

14

Ripened **RED** apples are picked at noon.

15

18

A coat of **RED** paint covers the old shed.

Tiny RED bugs fly around the pig's head.

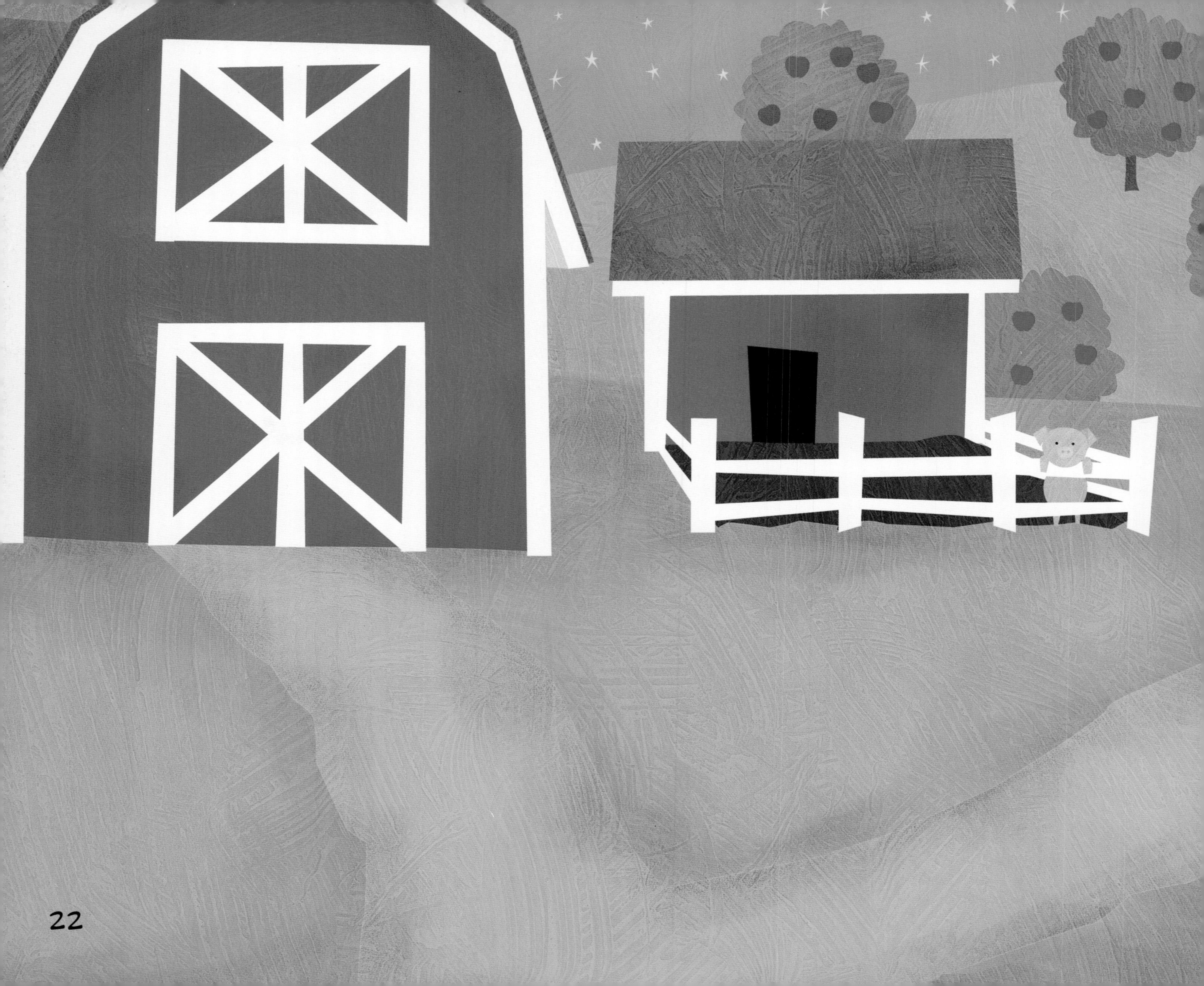

It's time for the farmer to go to bed.
What else on the farm is the color RED?

MAKE A RED COLLAGE

A collage is a collection of things. It is a work of art. To make one, look around your house and collect red items, such as ribbons, glitter, tissue paper, yarn, and pictures from old magazines. Then glue or tape your favorite red items to a sheet of red construction paper. You've made a red collage!

FUN FACTS

- Red is the most common color on national flags.

- Only male cardinals (a type of bird) are red. Female cardinals are reddish-brown.

- Stop signs weren't always red. The first stop sign was white with black letters.

- Red, orange, and yellow are called warm colors. Blue, green, and purple are called cool colors.

TO LEARN MORE

AT THE LIBRARY

Anderson, Moira. *Red*. Chicago: Raintree, 2006.

Gordon, Sharon. *Red*. New York: Benchmark Books, 2005.

Schuette, Sarah L. *Red*. Mankato, Minn.: A+ Books, 2003.

ON THE WEB

FactHound offers a safe, fun way to find Web sites related to this book. All of the sites on FactHound have been researched by our staff.

1. Visit www.facthound.com
2. Type in this special code: 140483110X
3. Click on the FETCH IT button.

Your trusty FactHound will fetch the best sites for you!

Look for all of the books in the Know Your Colors series:

Autumn Orange

Big Red Farm

Camping in Green

Hello, Yellow!

Purple Pride

Splish, Splash, and Blue

24